How Can I Deal with BULLYING?

A Book about Respect

SANDY DONOVAN

Lerner Publications Company • Minneapolis

Consultant:
Natasha Phillips, MA, Special Education
Special Education Teacher
at Beadle Elementary School
Yankton, South Dakota

Lerner Publications Company
A division of Lerner Publishing Group, Inc.
241 First Avenue North
Minneapolis, MN 55401 U.S.A.

For reading levels and more information, look up this title
at www.lernerbooks.com.

Library of Congress Cataloging-in-Publication Data

Donovan, Sandra, 1967–
    How can I deal with bullying? : a book about respect / by Sandy Donovan.
        pages   cm. — (Show your character)
    Includes index.
    ISBN 978–1–4677–1362–7 (lib. bdg. : alk. paper)
    ISBN 978–1–4677–2523–1 (eBook)
    1. Bullying—Juvenile literature. 2. Aggressiveness in children—Juvenile
literature. I. Title.
BF637.B85D65 2014
302.34'3—dc23   2013010879

Manufactured in the United States of America
1 – MG – 12/31/13

C. 1

TABLE OF CONTENTS

Have you seen bullying at your school? If you have seen someone make another person feel sad or hurt, over and over, then you have seen bullying.

Dealing with bullying is hard. It can make you mad—and sad. But dealing with bullying can be easier if you remember to **use respect**.

That means you remember to treat others as you would like to be treated. You use good manners. And you don't hit or use bad language.

The next time you have to deal with bullying, try doing so with respect. We'll give you a few tips to **help you on your way**.

4

Always treat others as you would like to be treated.

The next time she pushes you, tell her to stop. Say it in a firm voice.

If you don't feel safe telling her to stop, tell an adult. Or if she doesn't listen to you, you'll also need to tell an adult. You could ask the adult to keep an eye on the line. You can ask in private.

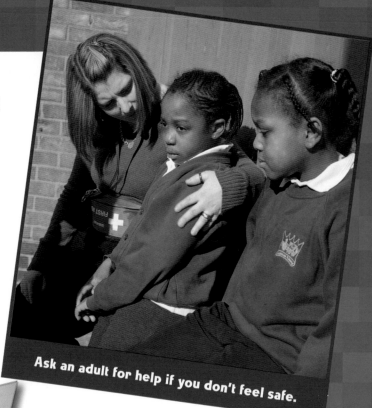

Ask an adult for help if you don't feel safe.

Did You Know?
Pushing, shoving, and hitting are kinds of physical bullying.

7

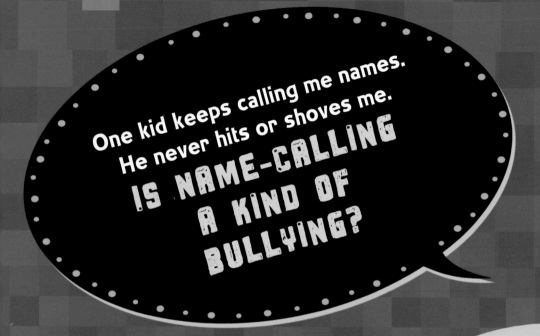

One kid keeps calling me names. He never hits or shoves me. IS NAME-CALLING A KIND OF BULLYING?

Yes!
If someone calls you names over and over, that's bullying. Teasing is bullying too.

Experts call this **verbal bullying**. Think of it as word bullying. No one gets hit. No one gets shoved. But someone does get hurt.

9

You can
stand up to word bullying
with **respect**.

Standing up for yourself with respect means that you don't call names back. You don't yell or insult. And you don't use bad language either. Instead, **speak politely but firmly**. Be clear and loud without shouting. That makes you a leader.

If the person still calls you names, tell an adult.

I'm best friends with Kaylee. But I'm also friends with Tess. Now Kaylee says she won't play with me at recess if I talk to Tess. **IS MY BEST FRIEND BULLYING ME?**

Yes!
Anyone who tells you who to be friends with is not acting like a friend. Kaylee is trying to control you. And if Tess heard what Kaylee said to you, then Kaylee would be making Tess feel bad too. That's bullying.

Experts call this **relational bullying**. That's a complicated way of saying that one person is trying to control another person.

So what should I say to Kaylee?

You can tell Kaylee that you don't want to make Tess feel bad. **You can use the word** *respect*. Say, "I want to respect Tess's feelings." You can say, "Leaving people out is mean. I wouldn't want to be left out." Maybe this will make Kaylee think about her actions.

You can also tell Kaylee that it's not fair of her to ask you to choose. Tell her that makes you feel bad.

True friends respect you when you're honest about your feelings.

But I don't want to mess up my friendship with Kaylee. If I just don't play with Tess, Kaylee will be happy. WHY CAN'T I JUST GO ALONG WITH MY FRIEND?

If you ignore Tess to hang out with Kaylee, you probably won't feel very good. Plus, Tess will be hurt.

You can tell Kaylee that you want to be friends with Tess. You can show others that you like Tess. And you can show them that you're not afraid of Kaylee. Other kids might follow your example of how to be a good friend.

Ignoring someone is hurtful. It can be a form of bullying.

18

Many times, there are three people—or even more—involved in bullying. The first is the person who bullies. The second is the person being bullied. And the third is anyone who knows it's happening.

Your actions can show bullies that they don't have power.

Guess who has the most power out of those people? (Hint: it's not the person who bullies.) It's the people who know it's happening. They are the ones with the **power to stand up to bullying**.

But I'm just a kid. WHEN I SEE BULLYING, HOW CAN I STOP IT?

People who see or know about bullying are called bystanders. Bystanders have two choices: they can *stand by*, or they can *stand up*.

Standing by means "doing nothing." It's the easiest thing to do. But it lets people get away with bullying. And that means people get hurt.

Standing up means "taking action." That could mean saying something to the person who's bullying. It could mean being friendly to the person being bullied. And it always means telling an adult if standing up doesn't stop the bullying. By doing these things, you are showing that bullying doesn't win.

Helping someone who is being bullied is a way to stand up to bullies.

At school, there's a kid named Jack who has a lot of friends. He always teases Jacob, who's new to our class and doesn't know many people. Everyone laughs, but I feel bad for Jacob.

BUT IF I SAY SOMETHING, WON'T I GET TEASED?

Jacob's in a tough spot. It must be awful to have everyone laugh at you. He also has to deal with the stress of being new, and that's never easy. That you feel bad shows you know right from wrong. Good for you!

You can say something to Jack. Tell him you don't like what he's doing. Tell him that it's wrong to tease another person.

So should I talk to Jack in private? Or in front of Jacob? Or in front of everyone?

If you're friends with Jack, you might want to talk to him in private. It can be more comfortable bringing up a serious issue with a friend when you're one-on-one.

If Jack isn't a buddy of yours, you might say something in front of others. There can be safety in numbers. Other kids just might be impressed by your bravery and join you in sticking up for Jacob.

Sometimes it's easier to talk to a friend one-on-one.

Stick up for others. You may find that lots of people will join you!

25

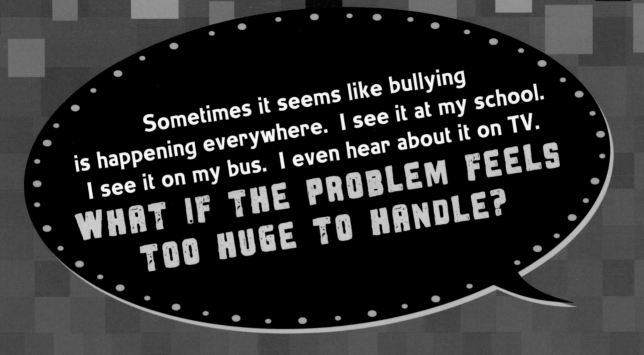

Sometimes it seems like bullying is happening everywhere. I see it at my school. I see it on my bus. I even hear about it on TV.

WHAT IF THE PROBLEM FEELS TOO HUGE TO HANDLE?

Bullying can feel like a huge problem. And there's no question that it's tough to deal with. But you have more power to stop bullying than you think. It often just takes one person brave enough to stand up to bullying. Soon others will join too.

Take the first step today. Tell people you don't like bullying. Be kind to someone who's being bullied. Little actions make a big difference.

Ask a teacher to help you too. Maybe you can start an antibullying club. Brainstorm ideas to keep your school bully-free. By working together, we can stomp out bullying!

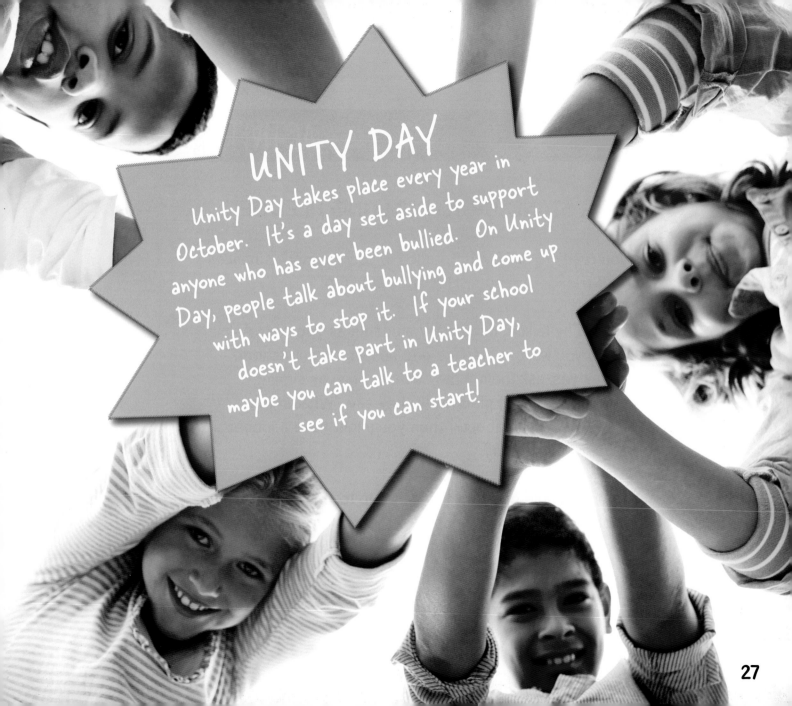

UNITY DAY

Unity Day takes place every year in October. It's a day set aside to support anyone who has ever been bullied. On Unity Day, people talk about bullying and come up with ways to stop it. If your school doesn't take part in Unity Day, maybe you can talk to a teacher to see if you can start!

MAKE A STAND UP TO BULLYING PLEDGE

Are you ready to make a difference in your school? Chances are, your friends and other kids are ready too!

Get started by talking to as many students as you can. Ask them, "Do you want to help me end bullying at our school?" If they say yes, ask them if they want to start by signing a Stand Up to Bullying pledge. (If they say, "What in the world are you talking about?" then you might have a longer conversation with them!)

Here's an example of how your Stand Up to Bullying pledge might look. If you want, you can use this one word for word. You can also make up your own.

I, (your name here), pledge to stand up to bullying whenever I see it.

I pledge to treat all kids—even people who bully—with respect.

I pledge to be polite and considerate to everyone.

I pledge to use good manners.

I pledge to not use bad language.

I pledge to not threaten, hit, or hurt anyone.

I pledge to be tolerant and accepting of differences.

I pledge to deal peacefully with anger, insults, and disagreements.

I pledge to tell people that I don't like bullying.

Signed: _____

Date: _____

bullying: making someone feel hurt, afraid, or uncomfortable over and over again

bystander: a person who sees or knows about bullying but is not the person bullying or the person being bullied

physical bullying: bullying by doing things such as pushing, shoving, and hitting

relational bullying: bullying by trying to control another person. In relational bullying, someone might refuse to talk to someone else, spread lies or rumors about someone, or try to make someone do things that he or she doesn't want to do.

respect: consideration or courtesy. If you treat someone with respect, you treat him or her as you would like to be treated.

verbal bullying: bullying with words, including teasing, name-calling, or insulting

FURTHER INFORMATION

Bullies: What Is Bullying?
http://pbskids.org/itsmylife/friends/bullies
Visit this site from PBS Kids for lots of information about the three different types of bullying.

Criswell, Patti Kelly. *Stand Up for Yourself and Your Friends: Dealing with Bullies and Bossiness and Finding a Better Way*. Middleton, WI: American Girl Publishing, 2009.
Get tips and advice from girls who have stood up for themselves and their friends in this American Girl book.

Golus, Carrie. *Take a Stand!: What You Can Do about Bullying*. Minneapolis: Lerner Publications, 2009.
Read more about how you can deal with bullying in this fun and interesting book.

Goodstein, Phyllis Kaufman, and Elizabeth Verdick. *Bystander Power: Now with Anti-Bullying Action*. Minneapolis: Free Spirit Publishing, 2012.
Learn more about the power of bystanders in this title.

Kids against Bullying
http://www.pacerkidsagainstbullying.org
This website from the PACER Center has lots of fun activities and games to help you learn more about bullying. The site also has videos of celebrity kids talking about bullying.

INDEX

PHOTO ACKNOWLEDGMENTS

The images in this book are used with the permission of: © Bubbles Photolibrary/Alamy, p. 4; © iStockphoto .com/CEFutcher, p. 5; © iStockphoto.com/Fly_Fast, p. 6; © Gideon Mendel/In Pictures/CORBIS, p. 7; © iStockphoto.com/monkeybusinessimages, pp. 9, 23; © Uwe Umstatter/Radius Images/Getty Images, p. 10; © Cusp/SuperStock, p. 11; © iStockphoto.com/Maria Pavlova, pp. 13, 17; © Patrick Molnar/CORBIS, p. 14; © iStockphoto.com/Alija, p. 15; © iStockphoto.com/fstop123, p. 18; © mother image/Digital Vision/Getty Images, p. 19; © Richard Nelson/Dreamstime.com, p. 20; © PhotoAlto/SuperStock, p. 21; © Sam Edwards/OJO Images/ Getty Images, p. 24; © Nick White/Photodisc/Getty Images, p. 25; © iStockphoto.com/GlobalStock, p. 27.

Front Cover: © Monkey Business Images/the Agency Collection/Getty Images.

Main body text set in ChurchwardSamoa Regular. Typeface provided by Chank.